Can't Handle Failure

Poet Stevens

CAN'T HANDLE FAILURE

iUniverse books may be ordered through booksellers or by contacting:

iUniverse
1663 Liberty Drive
Bloomington, IN 47403
www.iuniverse.com
844-349-9409

ISBN: 978-1-5320-8793-6 (sc)
ISBN: 978-1-5320-8794-3 (e)

Library of Congress Control Number: 2021917165

Print information available on the last page.

iUniverse rev. date: 08/30/2021

Contents

Eight year side chick

Yes I'm the side chick.

There is no shame.

I wanted the man, so

I played the game.

Three months in and

he sees me when he can,

but I have no shame. I'm

the side chick,

and I have no shame;

so I play the game.

One year ends, and he tells me that my pussy's the best.

No main chick status,

but I still play the game

because I want the man.

Two years in and he says he loves me,

but he won't leave her.

I want the man,

so I played the man.

Three years in and he's still with her,

but he says he loves me.

He just can't leave her because of the kids.

Four years in and he married her.

How could he marry her??

What about me?!

He tattooed her name on him,

but he says he loves me.

So I play the game

because I'm the number one side chick.

So I'll continue to play it the same.

Year six and seven they're having problems.

Maybe my chance is coming up.

Well they separated, so let me slide my way in.

He posted about me on his social media.

So now its year eight, and

he has a female friend. Oh

hell naw!

She's not about to push me out of my spot!

I worked too hard to be where I am!

Well technically, I'm still the side chick

because he's still married.

But I'll be damned if she tries to take my place! I've

played the game for so long and I want the man, so

he had to choose between her or me.

I'm the eight year side chick,

and I want the man.

I play the game.

He chose me so I won the game.

I was the eight year side chick,

and I have no shame.

I be petty with the friend; making her mad

because I was the eight year side chick,

and I had no shame.

I wanted the man and I played the game;

I will not lose him to the next.

I was an eight year side chick.

And I had no shame.

The game is checkers and I'm playing chess.

I was the eight year side chick,

and I had no shame.

I wanted the man,

and I won the game.

Changed

I lay awake at night and wonder who is lying next to

me.

You claim to be the same person,

but I don't think so.

I remember your touch was never this soft; gentle

like you're enjoying every inch of my body. Slowly

rubbing your fingertips against the crease of

my back; slowly up and down.

So warm and careful,

but you claim you're the same person.

Your kiss is so sweet and passionate,

no more pecks on the cheek.

Just you staring me into my eyes-

telling me you love me.

Slowly taking your lips and pressing them against

mine.

Feeling chills when we kiss,

everything including time stops when we're kissing.

You claim you're the same person.

I want to believe you,

but you're not the same.

So, if you're not the same person

I don't want the old you back.

But if you changed for me, thank you.

Cookies and Water

Have you ever felt like a ghost?

Just wondering around,

never finding peace?

That was me until I met you.

From the day you gave a complete stranger a hug,

I knew you were meant for me.

Then time took over, and we split.

But you always held a place in my heart.

Time went on and I faded away;

just like a ghost,

slowly fading away.

Then one day as I was wondering,

What if we met again?

Never knew some cookies and two bottles of water

would bring me love.

Those cookies reminded me of my heart,

soft and loveable to the right person.

Two bottles of water reminded me of you.

Refreshing and cool enough to put the fire of hatred in

my heart out.

Cookies and two bottles of water to find love.

A sweet tooth and your thirst; put two people at the right

place and the right time!

Cookies and water.

Extinction of a Community

Extinction of a community.

Let me tell you what it means to me.

You can't spell community without spelling unity,

and you can't spell unity without you and I.

So why are you and I watching this building we call a

community fall without making repairs?

There is a child walking around with the weight of

the world on his shoulders,

feeling like nobody cares.

What about the man who just got out of jail,

Who just wants a second chance?

Or the girl who just needs a father figure in her life?

The young lady everybody calls a thot

Who has a real life goal is to move out of the ghetto?

But nobody wants to help her except one teacher.

This isn't your hood or your block.

This is your community whether you want it or not!

So why bust shots?

Putting people's lives in danger; and for what?

To say you bout that life!

What about the lady in the community

Who was sleep and lost her life

because the bullet went astray? Now

her family hurts-

Another youth's life is wasted.

And why?

We couldn't work out our "he say, she say"

so there was no unity.

All of us are guilty

for this extinction of the community.

Fantasy

I'm lusting after someone who's not mine.

I don't want all your time just some,

A little attention can go so far.

Just a little time to see who you really are.

No games; no fronts.

NO physical contact unless you want.

Just a small step into your world.

I know that's not possible,

because you have so many girls.

Also you have a main chick,

and I have a man.

Just a little time with you-

Can't you understand?

I'm not your size zero barbie;

I don't have hood rat ways.

I'm really starting to feel like that maybe

If you got to know me deeper than my outer

layer.

But I choose to play

So I'll save my little fantasy

Fat Girl

The way I feel has nothing to do with you

It's just me.

I don't know the woman in the mirror.

She seems so sad; with a bright smile.

Her eyes are so dark and lonely.

That smile copied and pasted.

This body-oh this body!

Just fat with stretch marks.

Always being told you can't be beautiful because you're

fat.

Shopping seems like a punishment because nothing fits.

Everybody says if you stop feeding your face

You can lose weight.

Well then I'll starve myself. That

doesn't work.

You can exercise and change your diet.

That doesn't work either.

So you google ways to lose weight,

but all people are telling you

is to take this pill; buy this wrap.

Get this waist trainer.

I get all this stuff, And

nothing is working!

I'm seeing all these pretty woman, And I

see him side eye and look at them. Every

last one of them

prettier than me!

All of them a perfect size and a perfect face.

Nothing in the wrong place!

That's a punch in the stomach.

I'm out of shape with acne.

I feel less than a woman;

I'm having nightmares of you leaving me

For women who are in better shape.

Why am I this ugly fat girl

That everybody looks down on?!?

Stupid fat girl.

Fear

For we can rule a nation with fear.

Our bills are a good example.

If we don't pay our lights,

We have a fear of being in the dark.

Alone with our own demons; Dancing

in fear of them taking over. Showing us

the should have and would

have beens.

Our fear of being alone.

No one to vent to or express our feelings

to.

The fear of regret.

Knowing or thinking that you could've

been.

But your fear of failure stopped you from

being the best.

Don't let your fear stop you from

speaking against what's wrong.

That would make you the bad guy also

because you didn't stop it or speak

against it.

Don't let your fear be the reason for

anything.

Be great and fearless.

Be great and fearless!

Fourth Eye Blind

My head is aching from all the pain that you caused.

Numb from it all.

It's to the point,

I'm fourth eye blind.

This is that one eye I wish I could take away.

It does what it wants, And

cries from pain. Ripping my

soul into pieces

because it wants to see the good in people.

And for what?

They always seem good,

but then their true colors show.

That eye is so color blind to it.

It let history repeat itself over and over again;

I'm tired of the foolishness.

Tired of the lies.

But it continues

because I'm fourth eye blind.

Growing up

So many things I want to know, There

are so many places I want to go. So

many lessons I have learned,

In many ways than one.

I've lost so much,

And gained a whole lot more.

I gave so much love,

And had some took.

I've been close to death,

And I wasn't shook.

I've always had protection,

And I know not to fear.

I've had friends come and go,

I've been called retard and slow.

I've made it through rapes,

Because I will make it;

No more fakes.

I do what I please

He might have taken a piece of me,

but he didn't take the whole me.

I refuse to let you take my life.

I have so many jobs left to do;

A friend, mother, and maybe a wife.

So I forgave,

And let my past stay behind.

Because no ghost will haunt my life.

I gotta grow up like a big kid getting rid of his tricycle.

Help Me

Sometimes I wish this was all a dream.

All these things are attacking me like a team.

I'm trying to sort everything out,

But I can't seem to figure it out.

I'm fighting all my demons.

They travel in groups;

Ready to jump me.

I'm trying to fight my demons.

Old wounds that should have healed; Those

demons came out from being sealed. My

regrets of life

here and ready to play.

I'm trying to fight my demons.

"Be calm", they say.

"Don't worry, just pray." I'm

still fighting my demons.

They don't fight fair.

Who are you to tell me how I'm supposed to

feel?

Am I not supposed to be sad because I carry this

smile?

Am I not supposed to shed a tear when I'm sad;

Or am I supposed to walk around Heartless and

cold to the world?

So if I'm not supposed to feel,

what am I to do?

Sit here like and ice queen

And feel nothing.

But I do feel!

And I hurt!

I'm really hurt; help me please!

Somebody please help me!

Hollow

Some days I wish I could take this heart of

mine out of my body.

It's causing me so much pain!

I'm starting to feel as hollow as a chocolate

Easter bunny.

Why must it take so many blows and keep

moving?

As a soldier in a battle that he knows he

can't win;

But he won't give up because he believes he

can win.

Even against all odds, he just won't give up.

This heart of mine has a mind of its own.

Wishing for one of those fairy tale endings;

The ones read to girls where the prince

comes and saves the day and they live

happily ever after.

But then reality hits and I go back to

existing,

not living again because it feels like I'm

being buried alive.

I'm fighting back; just taking the blows as

my slave ancestors.

Just blow after blow with no stop.

This heart of mine has so many scares that I

don't think it will ever heal.

Like a bad memory from your past that you

just want to forget.

Oh love, why must you play with my heart

strings?

Just act right and do the right thing like give

up, forget it and leave it be.

Because when I think I'm happy you make a

fool of me.

Hypothetically

What if I told you I fell for someone that wasn't

you.

Hypothetically.

And he touches me in ways you used to.

Hypothetically.

And I had sex with him and he felt like you.

Hypothetically.

And he told me he loved me and I started to love

him too.

Hypothetically. And

I got pregnant.

Hypothetically.

And he was excited because he was going to be

a daddy.

But so was you.

Hypothetically.

I have a baby.

And you're a great dad.

Doing everything a great dad is supposed to do.

He doesn't want anything to do with the baby.

He just wanted the title of daddy.

Hypothetically.

Now our son is five and he's not looking like you,

but you're not questioning it because it's your son.

He creeps back into the picture, because

things aren't going right in his life.

Hypothetically.

Now the street crew is talking and you're

hearing the rumors.

You ignore them

And continue to take care of our son.

Then he comes to you and talk;

Man to man. Hypothetically.

So you rush home to confront me about what he

told you.

You know it's not a lie because he even tells you

about that certain spot that makes me hot.

That spot only you know about.

Hypothetically.

I cry and confess that what he told you was true.

But I never loved him; I only loved you.

I also throw up the fact that the baby I'm

pregnant with is yours.

Why did he wait five years to come into our

son's life?

At the end of the day

You're his daddy; the only man who has ever

been there for him

You're mad and hurt.

This I know.

I hurt you for five years; knowing our baby might

not be yours.

Hypothetically.

You want to leave but you don't want to just

leave our son.

So you stay but things are strained.

We walk past each other but the looks aren't the

same.

We sleep in different rooms.

We play our roles for the kids.

Could we ever go back to being the same?

Hypothetically of course.

Last Night Dream

As I slept, I had a dream.

I dreamt of real love.

Not the same "I love you" I hear

everyday.

But real love.

Where his touch sends chills down my

spine.

The love you read about in romance

novels.

The kind of love where his kiss is like

heaven.

And to be away from you is hell.

The kind where phone conversations go

on for hours.

And I think of you in the shower.

The kind where I daydream about us

being a family.

I'm your wife and you're my husband.

The kind where I see us growing old

together.

And you finally met my mother.

Where you take me as I am;

My good and my flaws.

The kind where you still love me, even

when my hair isn't done and I'm walking

around in a bra.

The kind where we make love for hours,

not minutes.

We put all our feelings in it.

Then I awake and find it's just a dream.

But one day I will find you

My sweet gentle king.

Like a slave

Sometimes the world makes you feel like a slave.

We wake up to repeat the same patterns over and over

again.

Somedays, I want to run away to my land of freedom.

But master always finds and beats me with a new job and

many things I don't think I can handle.

The whole time I'm plotting my freedom.

I leave one night and I'm off to my freedom land.

Lord please watch over me as I make this journey.

So many snakes in the grass; they told the master I'm

gone.

So now the hunt is on.

Will I make it or will he find me?

Lost

When you've lost everything,

You start to feel and see darkness that no light can out

shine.

You adapt to that darkness to the point of living in it is no

problem.

You wander around like a lost soul; waiting on the end to

come; but every day is a disappointment.

The end never comes and again you're wondering.

Doomed to feel all the pain, but also a lifeless vessel.

Pain is all you feel; so deep but never leaves visible

marks.

Just a deep wound on the heart.

Missing Piece

I feel like a piece of me is missing and I don't know what

it is.

I pray every night for a sign; to know what's missing.

This void is keeping me from enjoying my days as a

blessed, beautiful woman.

Maybe I need to do a self check because I'm afraid.

I never gave my whole heart to anyone

But one person and it didn't work out. So

now I feel like a child lost in Wal- Mart.

I could just walk to the front and ask someone to call my

parents.

But me being the control freak that I am.

I have to find my parents on my own,

No matter how long it will take. The

same with my heart.

But it seems the more I try to keep you out the more I

can't help letting you in.

Oh love stop making a fool of me

Missing You

Why did you leave me

In the worst way.

You died and I never got a chance to say I love you.

You were more than a grandfather, you were my

friend.

You've been with me through thick and thin,

That's why it's hard to believe you're gone.

I remember when I was little,

You used to hum a song; I never knew the title.

There was never a day you didn't have a smile.

Wishing and wondering;

Why did you have to go and leave me in this world

feeling alone and cold?

Your favorite color was yellow;

Mine are pink and blue.

I want you to know one thing,

I still miss you.

My letters to God

My tears are my letters to God.

Why must I hurt;

What trial must I complete?

My troubles are long,

My pain is strong.

So I write my letters to God.

Each tear is a trouble.

A stress; a trial that I feel like I can't handle.

So I wait until I'm alone.

I write my letters to God. No

interruptions, no phone.

No facebook, snapchat, or google.

Just me and my letters to God.

My Life

It's my life and I refuse to lose.

This guy's going to kill me;

It's my life though.

He has a gun pointed at my head;

And it's loaded ready to be pulled.

It's my life though.

He's screaming if I don't want to be with him,

He's going to kill me then himself.

It's my life though.

He's screaming "Do you want to be with me?"

I'm screaming for help.

Wrong answer.

Bam!

Two fists and a gun hit me.

It's my life though.

He says "I'll never hit you again,

Just say you want to be with me."

I scream "NO! Let me go!"

Wrong answer.

Now I'm being pushed down the stairs.

I'm trying to get up so I can run,

But he's over me; yanking at my clothes

It's my life though.

"If you don't say you will be with me,

I'm going to rape you and kill you."

It's my life though.

I've got to stop being something I can't be, which is a

victim.

I'm strong for a reason.

I'm better than this! Looking him

straight into the eyes; I say "Either

kill me or leave,

Because I refuse to take another hit!"

It's my life and you're not in it!

Second Hand Healthcare

Why must I wait so long to be seen at the

hospital?

Is it because I have no health care

insurance?

Why are my health care needs guessed

upon with no tests or labs to back it up?

Because I have no insurance.

Why do people with money and benefits go

before me; I've been waiting six hours to be

seen.

Because I have no insurance.

Why when I say my side hurts, you tell me

it's an UTI and don't check anything?

Because I have no insurance.

Why when I tell you my baby's sick you tell

me it's a cold?

Now we're back with a fever of 103 and he's

being rushed to the back with tubes and

oxygen.

And why?

Because I have no insurance. Healthcare

is supposed to be equal for all

people.

But that's some bullshit!

Good healthcare goes to the people with

healthcare insurance or cash.

I don't have either of those.

So I get treated like a colored person in the

1940's.

Backdoor healthcare for all us poor folks.

Selfish

We made a choice,

In which we thought it was good.

Now a couple years later,

I wonder how could I know

What I did was the right thing to do.

I'm being selfish because I want you back.

I wonder if you remember me?

Or is that picture gone too.

Your birthday comes and goes.

I would love to have you again,

But again I ask, am I being selfish?

I didn't have what you needed,

So when they found a family that did

I let you go.

But again I ask, am I being selfish for wanting you

back?

This part is true.

I see you growing up;

If only for five minutes.

It hurt me to know I let you go.

I did it to make sure you had all the things I couldn't

give you.

So the only question I keep asking is

Am I selfish for wanting you back Or

is that normal?

Simple love

Love is simple.

Love is kind.

When I met you, My

heart was blind. I

gave up on love.

I let my past live in my present.

Then I met you,

And you turned my life around.

We both had our doubts that this wouldn't last

Because of our past.

But we decided to take that leap,

And we landed here.

We met in a strange way,

And you told me you planned our future.

I asked how you planned for us when you doubted us.

And you answered "Because I knew both of us won't give

up that easily."

That part you never lied about.

Not matter how many times I wanted to quit because of

the times getting harder, you wouldn't let me

Never thought I would feel this way about anybody.

With you I can touch stars,

And swim the deepest ocean.

With you I can sing opera,

Or give a speech on peace.

I could stop a war, And

end world hunger. Our

love is that strong,

That part I know.

No matter how many people say we shouldn't be

together,

We stand together as one.

For the fact we can't live other people's lives,

Because some people don't want to be happy.

For they don't know what true happiness is,

Or maybe they don't want to let go of their past.

For we have all been hurt before.

We just have to learn to let go.

We love every gift that our present brings.

Whether it be sunlight or rain.

So this is to the one I love;

Who taught me to never let go and never give up on love.

Sometimes

Sometimes I wonder why I keep going under.

Is my heart too kind to help others; is my favorite

line.

Who takes care of me when I'm broken down and

crying?

I know the man upstairs is watching me and telling

me it's ok.

How can man be so cruel in this world?

My struggle is my motto.

Without you I don't know if I could've made this

change.

I'm glad it was raining so no one could see my tears.

So many to shed from all the years.

No drugs can heal my pain but I learned the art of

forgiveness.

Still I feel the same.

What am I to do when it's sunny outside but all I feel is

blue?

I need no street creds for I don't like people in my

business.

So can I get a witness for trying to stay legal?

Miss Peaches is my alter ego, Who

wants to come out and turn up.

She wants to give everybody who caused us pain the

same.

But that would leave us nowhere.

Just a temporary satisfaction; but the reaction of all

this could lead to real trouble with no help.

So who helps the person who helps everyone who

needs it in her path?

No one; they just laugh for they're thinking it's not

me; so why should I care?

I start looking in the mirror, not knowing who is

there.

I stare hoping she will tell me who she is.

She stresses and cries so much I really don't notice

her face.

All I see is her tears.

She just keeps looking at me wishing the pain would

go away.

I figured who the woman looking back at me was me.

Stripped

When your heart is stripped of all feelings you start

to feel like a hollow being.

A nobody; like the video game Kingdom hearts.

Nobody who just wants to feel whole again.

Nobodys don't sleep or eat.

They're just there and wish they could be real

humans.

Barely eating; they just get up and do the same thing

everyday.

Like a DVD on repeat.

Oh to be whole again.

To feel normal.

To feel love. To

feel human.

Stuck

Stuck in a love song.

Where the beat and the words are wrong.

No shapes; no feelings.

Is this really the reason

Why sleeping with you feel like I'm freezing?

Cold shoulders along with cold words.

You say you love me. Such

a thoughtless phrase.

You got games so play them; don't play me.

You see I'm young but not dumb.

I've been through too much.

I can tell the difference; even in your touch.

Your love is gone.

Be careful who you leave scorn.

For my love is deep, And

has always been true.

When you had nothing;

I always had you.

But now you got bread,

And other women opened their beds and their legs.

Be careful who you leave scorn.

Now you're back to nothing,

And I'm so gone.

Thank you

Thank you for being you.

You're a selfish, inconsiderate self- proclaiming

bastard.

How could you ever treat me like a second rate

citizen?

Never in my life have I ever let a poor hustler

play with me.

It never really bothered me until I went to think

about who was there when you fell.

Answer that.

Who was there when you couldn't handle life?

You wanted to kill yourself.

Do you have an answer for that?

When you got sick and your crowd went away.

Answer that!

I've been everything to you.

From your friend, nurse, cook, pharmacist,

counselor, and uber.

But I guess that doesn't mean shit compared to

the people who don't mean shit!

But they're ready to jump and fight for your last

name.

But when you was sick they left faster than a

deadbeat dad.

This is the last time!

I let this happen to my heart.

I'm taking the same knife you stabbed me with

to cut you out of my life.

So thank you for releasing me.

Thank you.

To My Son Zane

I never thought the love of my life would weigh less than

six pounds.

During my first month I didn't know.

My second month, my moods started to show.

My third month I got to hear your heartbeat.

The fourth month, I got to see what I thought was a girl.

My fifth month, I got worried and prayed. My

sixth month, I got to say I'm having a boy!

While it's winding towards the end he kicks, and smiles;

and I'm always hungry.

My eighth month, he had a name.

I went for a night stroll and you came the next day.

Weighing five pounds four ounces and a wonderful

eighteen inches tall.

In my heart it was like one-hundred pounds of love had sat

here and stayed.

Now you're growing up and I still feel the same.

I love you my son.

I love you Zane.

True Game

You swear you're balling.

We call it tricking.

You could've jack your dick and kept that money.

But you swear you're winning.

You're simple; like an addition.

Now, you got me over here wishing

On a star and broken heart scars,

That I never met you.

You swear you're running game,

But you're the fool.

Sit down and listen to the old cats.

They can tell you the rules of the game you're trying to

run on me.

I've been in the game longer.

Pimp game stronger than the concrete around your feet.

I scheme while you sleep.

But now your learning

Like a child sticking paper in fire; screaming its burning!

But now I'm *gone,*

And you're sad and alone.

Undercover Abuse

I'm crying while I'm filled with nightmares.

I see images when I'm awake as if they

were still there so fresh in my mind.

Never wanting that to happen a second or

third time; seems like nobody understands

me.

So I pray dear lord please take this pain

away.

I need some real help, but I don't have any

real friends.

What's really going on in my mind?

Have I actually lost it?

Dear Lord, please don't let me lose it!

So this is my cry or my plea for help.

Just thought I would let you know what's on

my mind some days.

What happened to us

What happened to us?

When was being a size 2 the only way I could become

sexy?

When was twerking videos more important than

education?

Why does my color determine my life expectancy?

Where is the family structure?

What happened to us?

Why are there veterens coping with demons and

homeless, going without the help they deserve from us?

Why is a wall so important that it means millions will go

without pay, food, shelter and medical help?

What's really happened to us?

How is it the less clothes I got on the more attention I

get;

And people listen to me.

If I cover up I'm considered basic and lame.

What happened to us?

If you have an opinion and others don't agree

Your social media gets blocked!

What happened to us?

Are we that soft of a nation to where

If you say nothing your good,

But if you speak you're bad?

What happened to us?

Printed in the United States
by Baker & Taylor Publisher Services